D1203395

How Toys Bounce

Helen Whittaker

Smart Apple Media
P.O. Box 3263
Mankato, MN, 56002

First published in 2011 by
MACMILLAN EDUCATION AUSTRALIA PTY LTD
15–19 Claremont Street, South Yarra 3141

Visit our website at www.macmillan.com.au or go directly to www.macmillanlibrary.com.au

Associated companies and representatives throughout the world.

Library of Congress Cataloging-in-Publication Data has been applied for.

Publisher: Carmel Heron
Commissioning Editor: Niki Horin
Managing Editor: Vanessa Lanaway
Editors: Emma de Smit and Tim Clarke
Proofreader: Helena Newton
Designer: Kerri Wilson
Page layout: Romy Pearse
Photo researcher: Wendy Duncan (management: Debbie Gallagher)
Illustrator: Ned Culic
Production Controller: Vanessa Johnson

Manufactured in China by Macmillan Production (Asia) Ltd.
Kwun Tong, Kowloon, Hong Kong
Supplier Code: CP March 2011

Acknowledgements

The publisher would like to thank Heidi Ruhnau, Head of Science at Oxley College, Victoria, for her assistance in reviewing manuscripts.

The author and publisher are grateful to the following for permission to reproduce copyright material:

Front cover photograph: Girl bouncing basketball © Getty Images/Taxi/Jade Albert Studio, Inc.

Photographs courtesy of: 123rf/Dmitry Naumov, 6; Corbis/Eyetrigger Pty Ltd, 4 (bottom left), /Randy Faris, 9 (bottom left), 14, /Simon Marcus, 5 (right); Getty Images/Kate Connell, 8 (right), 12, /Taxi/Jade Albert Studio, Inc., 1; iStockphoto/Don Nichols, 20 (right), /kk88, 9 (top), 16, /sonyae, 8 (left), 10; Masterfile, 5 (left); MEA Images/Image Source, 4 (bottom centre); photolibrary/Alamy/Aurora Photos, 4 (bottom right); Pixmac/Yuri Arcurs, 4 (top left); Shutterstock/cassiede alain, 4 (top right), /Michael William, 4 (top centre), /Thomas M Perkins, 9 (right), 18, /Larry Wolfe, 20 (left).

While every care has been taken to trace and acknowledge copyright, the publisher tenders their apologies for any accidental infringement where copyright has proved untraceable. They would be pleased to come to a suitable arrangement with the rightful owner in each case.

Contents

When a word is printed in **bold**, you can look up its meaning in the Glossary on page 31.

Toys and Forces

Forces make toys work. Forces make toys start moving, change direction, speed up, slow down, and stop moving. Forces also change the shape of some toys.

| Bouncing toys | Floating toys | Flying toys |
| Rolling toys | Sliding toys | Spinning toys |

None of these toys would work without forces.

What Is a Force?

A force is a push or a pull. When you push something, it moves away from you. When you pull something, it moves towards you.

When this girl applies a pushing force to the beach ball, it moves away from her.

When this boy applies a pulling force to the bag of soccer balls, it moves towards him.

How Does a Bouncing Toy Work?

A bouncing toy works when a pushing or pulling force makes it move. The toy moves by bouncing up and down. This happens because part of the toy changes shape.

You bounce when you jump on a jumping castle because a pushing force changes the castle's shape.

Part of a bouncing toy changes shape when a force acts on it. When the force stops, the toy changes back to its original shape.

1 child jumps down

2 child moves up

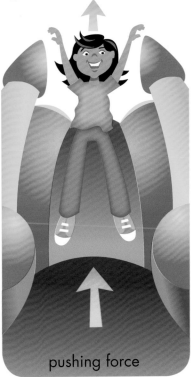

pushing force

pushing force

child's feet make jumping castle change shape

jumping castle changes back to its original shape

The pushing force of a child bouncing on a jumping castle changes its shape.

How Do Forces Make Bouncing Toys Work?

Different forces make bouncing toys work. Pushes and pulls make the toys work in different ways. Forces can make bouncing toys work in these ways.

Forces can make bouncing toys start moving.

Forces can make bouncing toys change direction.

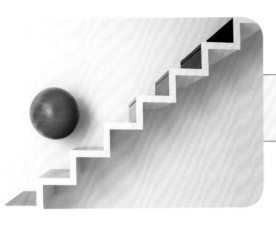

Forces can make bouncing toys speed up.

Forces can make bouncing toys slow down.

Forces can make bouncing toys stop moving.

What Makes a Bouncing Toy Start Moving?

When forces act on a bouncing toy, they can make it start moving. One force that can make a bouncing toy start moving is a pushing force.

A trampoline starts moving when you apply a pushing force with your feet.

Applying a pushing force makes part of a bouncing toy change shape. When the toy changes back to its original shape, it creates a force in the opposite direction.

1

springs change shape

pushing force
applied by feet

springs change back
to their original shape

2

A trampoline bounces because its **springs** change shape.

pushing force
applied by springs

What Makes a Bouncing Toy Change Direction?

When forces act on a bouncing toy, they can make it change direction. One force that can make a bouncing toy change direction is a pushing force.

A pushing force can make a pogo stick change direction.

A bouncing toy changes direction when a pushing force is applied to one side. The toy will turn in the direction of the push.

A pogo stick changes direction when a pushing force is applied to one side.

child leaning applies a pushing force to one side of the pogo stick

pushing force makes the pogo stick change direction as it bounces

What Makes a Bouncing Toy Speed Up?

When forces act on a bouncing toy, they can make it speed up. A pulling force called **gravity** can make bouncing toys speed up.

As the ball bounces down the stairs, the pulling force of gravity makes the ball speed up.

When a bouncing toy is on a slope, gravity pulls it downwards. This makes the toy speed up as it bounces down the slope.

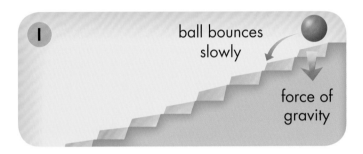

1 ball bounces slowly

force of gravity

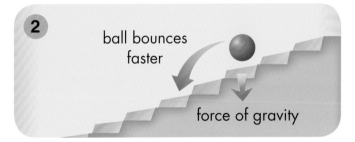

2 ball bounces faster

force of gravity

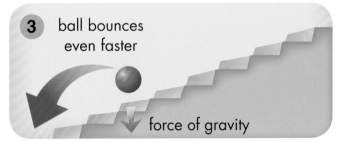

3 ball bounces even faster

force of gravity

The pulling force of gravity makes a ball speed up when bouncing down a slope.

What Makes a Bouncing Toy Slow Down?

When forces act on a bouncing toy, they can make it slow down. A pushing force called **air resistance** can make bouncing toys slow down.

The force of air resistance is making these bouncing mobiles slow down.

Air resistance is a pushing force that acts on an object as it moves through the air. Air resistance pushes against a bouncing object and makes it slow down.

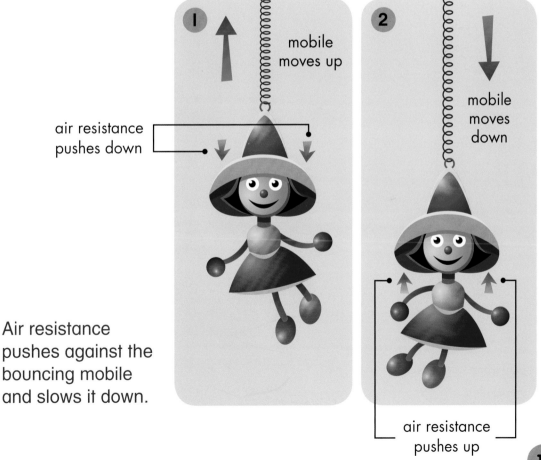

air resistance pushes down

1 mobile moves up

2 mobile moves down

air resistance pushes up

Air resistance pushes against the bouncing mobile and slows it down.

What Makes a Bouncing Toy Stop Moving?

When forces act on a bouncing toy, they can make it stop moving. One force that can make a bouncing toy stop moving is a pushing force.

You can make a space hopper stop bouncing by pushing against the ground with your feet.

18

One way to make a bouncing toy stop moving is to use a pushing force. A pushing force in the opposite direction to the toy's movement will make the toy stop moving.

When riding a space hopper, the force of pushing your feet against the ground will make the hopper stop moving.

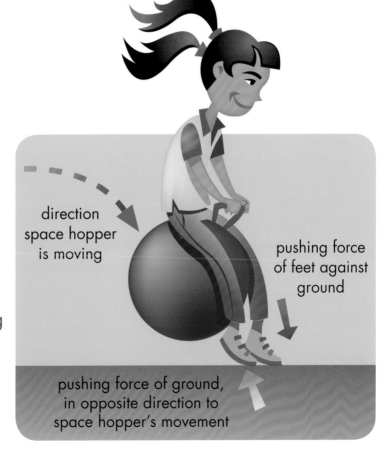

direction space hopper is moving

pushing force of feet against ground

pushing force of ground, in opposite direction to space hopper's movement

What Else Affects How a Bouncing Toy Moves?

Some bouncing toys are filled with air. The amount of air inside this sort of toy affects how high it can bounce.

A basketball full of air bounces higher than a basketball with not much air inside it.

a lot of air inside

not much air inside

When a bouncing toy is full of air, the air pushes outward with a large force. It changes back to its original shape quickly. This makes the toy bounce high.

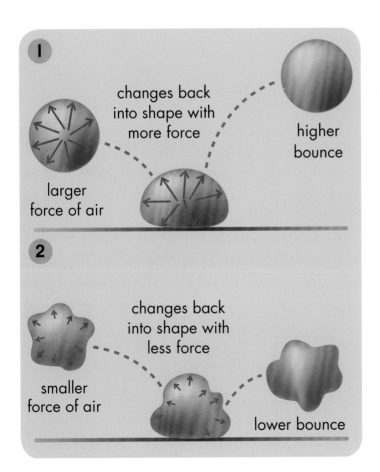

1

changes back into shape with more force

higher bounce

larger force of air

2

changes back into shape with less force

smaller force of air

lower bounce

The first basketball changes back to its original shape with more force and bounces higher.

Make a Bouncing Toy: Jack-in-the-box

This colorful jack-in-the-box is easy to make and fun to play with.

What you need:

- large matchbox
- colored paper
- scissors
- glue stick
- 3 pieces of different colored, letter-sized cardboard
- ruler
- pencil
- double-sided sticky tape

This jack-in-the-box has a cardboard spring that makes it bounce.

What to do:

1 Cut the colored paper into shapes. Decorate the matchbox by gluing on the colored shapes.

2 Measure the width of the box. Subtract ½ inch. This is the width of the spring strip.

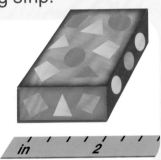

3 With the pencil and ruler, draw lines lengthwise on two pieces of the colored cardboard. Draw the strips the same width you figured in step 2.

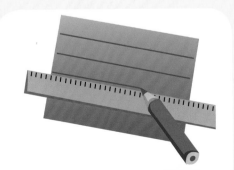

4 Cut two pieces of the colored cardboard into strips.

5 Join two cardboard strips at their corners with double-sided tape.

6 Fold the strips over one another. Keep repeating until you run out of cardboard.

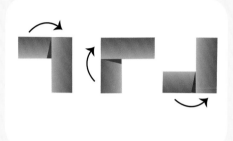

7 When you cannot make any more folds, join more strips using more double-sided tape.

8 Keep adding and folding strips of cardboard until the flattened cardboard spring is nearly the same height as the box.

9 Draw the jack-in-the-box's head and arms on the third piece of cardboard, then cut them out.

10 Tape the head and arms on top of the cardboard spring. Fold them as shown in the picture.

fold along dotted lines

11 Tape the bottom of the spring to the bottom of the inner box.

12 Press the cardboard spring down. Put the box inside its cover. Slide open the box for a fun surprise!

Experiment: How High Will It Bounce?

Try this experiment to find out how a ball's temperature affects how high it bounces.

What you need:
- 2 tennis balls
- freezer
- microwave oven
- oven mitt
- smooth, hard floor

Ask a parent or teacher for help.

What to do:

1 Put one of the tennis balls in the freezer for one hour.

2 Heat the other tennis ball in the microwave for 1 ½ minutes on high heat. Remove it carefully using the oven mitt.

3 Hold both tennis balls at the same height above a hard floor. Hold the hot ball with the oven mitt.

4 Let go of both tennis balls at the same time.

5 Watch the tennis balls as they fall and compare how high they bounce. What do you notice?

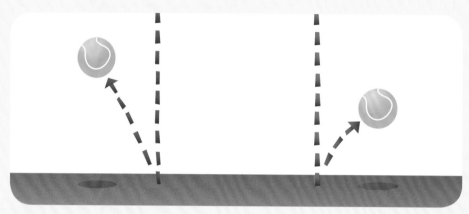

What happens?

You should find out that the cold tennis ball does not bounce as high as the warm one.

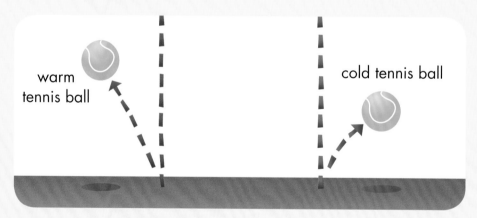

warm tennis ball

cold tennis ball

Why does it happen?

Tennis balls are filled with air. Warm air takes up more space than cold air. Warm air pushes outward on the inside of the ball with more force than cold air.

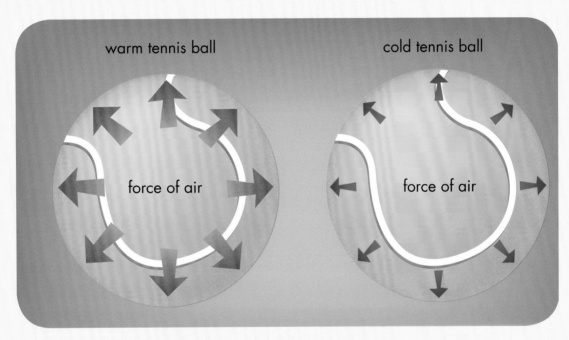

warm tennis ball

cold tennis ball

force of air

force of air

The warm ball changes back to its original shape with more force so it bounces higher.

The balls change shape when they hit the ground, then change back to their original shape.

How Forces Make Bouncing Toys Work

This table shows some of the pushing and pulling forces that act on bouncing toys.

Forces make toys ...	Pushing or pulling force?	Example of the force acting on a toy	
start moving	pushing force	A trampoline starts moving when a pushing force acts on it.	
change direction	pushing force	A pogo stick changes direction when a pushing force acts on one side.	
speed up	pulling force	A ball speeds up as it bounces down a slope because the pulling force of gravity is acting on it.	
slow down	pushing force	A bouncing mobile slows down when the pushing force of air resistance acts on it.	
stop moving	pushing force	A space hopper stops when a pushing force acts on it.	

Glossary

air resistance   a pushing force that acts on an object as it moves through the air, and slows down moving objects

bouncing   moving up and down

gravity   a pulling force that pulls objects toward Earth, and acts on everything, all the time

springs   metal coils that quickly move back to their original shape after they have been squashed or stretched

Index